Self discipline secret: Steps to achieve your dreams

Terry T. McClelland

Introduction

The ability to effectively control one's actions, emotions, and impulses is a critical quality of self-discipline. It's the discipline of choosing actions that support long-term objectives above transient cravings. This trait is necessary to succeed in a variety of spheres of life, such as relationships, work, education, and health.

Establishing precise objectives, making well-organised plans, and continuously carrying them out are all necessary for developing self-discipline. It calls for tenacity, endurance, and maintaining concentration in the face of difficulties and disappointments. Self-discipline promotes a sense of empowerment and control by assisting people in forming healthy habits and breaking bad ones.

Self-control can be incorporated into daily activities to increase overall contentment, productivity, and well-being. It enables people to make conscious decisions that support their long-term prosperity and personal development while being true to their beliefs and ideals. In the end, self-discipline is the cornerstone of realising one's potential and living a happy, purposeful life.

Chapter 1:Self discipline

Self-discipline is a critical trait that enables individuals to manage their behaviours, emotions, and desires in a way that aligns with their long-term goals and values. It is the capacity to stay focused and committed to a task or objective, even when faced with temptations, distractions, or challenges. This skill is essential for achieving success in various domains of life, including academics, career, health, and personal relationships.

At its core, self-discipline involves the ability to delay gratification. This means forgoing immediate pleasures or comforts in favour of more significant rewards that come from sustained effort and perseverance. For example, a student may choose to study for an upcoming exam instead of going out with friends, understanding that the long-term benefits of good grades and knowledge acquisition outweigh the short-term enjoyment of socialising.

Developing self-discipline begins with setting clear and attainable goals. These goals provide a roadmap for what one wants to achieve and serve as a constant reminder of why self-discipline is necessary. The process involves creating structured plans and routines that support these goals. For instance, an individual aiming to improve their physical fitness might set a goal to exercise a certain number of times per week and develop a workout schedule to follow.

Maintaining self-discipline requires a combination of intrinsic and extrinsic motivation. Intrinsic motivation comes from within and is driven by personal satisfaction and the joy of achieving a goal. Extrinsic motivation, on the other hand, involves external rewards such as praise, recognition, or financial incentives. Both types of motivation play a role in sustaining self-discipline over the long term.

Resilience and patience are also crucial components of self-discipline. Resilience enables individuals to bounce back from setbacks and continue working towards their goals despite difficulties. Patience helps them understand that meaningful achievements often take time and sustained effort. Together, these qualities help individuals remain steadfast in their pursuit of success, even when progress seems slow or obstacles arise.

Building self-discipline involves practising self-control, which is the ability to regulate one's emotions, thoughts, and behaviours. This can be challenging, especially in situations where immediate gratification is readily available. However, by consistently exercising self-control, individuals can strengthen their capacity for self-discipline. Techniques such as mindfulness, meditation, and positive self-talk can aid in developing greater self-control.

Self-discipline also entails the ability to prioritise tasks and manage time effectively. Time management skills are essential for balancing various responsibilities and ensuring that important tasks are completed on time. By organising tasks in order of importance and setting deadlines, individuals can create a structured approach to achieving their goals.

The benefits of self-discipline are far-reaching. In the realm of academics, self-discipline can lead to better study habits, higher grades, and a deeper understanding of the subject matter. In the workplace, it can result in increased productivity, better job performance, and career advancement. For personal health, self-discipline can lead to improved fitness, healthier eating habits, and overall well-being. In relationships, it can foster stronger connections through consistent effort and commitment.

Incorporating self-discipline into daily routines can significantly enhance one's quality of life. It fosters a sense of control and empowerment, allowing individuals to make deliberate choices that align with their values and aspirations. This, in turn, leads to greater overall satisfaction and fulfilment.

Ultimately, self-discipline is the foundation for achieving one's full potential. It is the driving force behind personal growth and success, enabling individuals to lead purposeful, goal-oriented lives. By cultivating self-discipline, individuals can navigate life's challenges with confidence and determination, continually striving to become the best version of themselves.

The power of mindful self-discipline

Mindful self-discipline combines the principles of mindfulness with the practice of self-discipline, creating a powerful synergy that enhances personal growth, productivity, and well-being. It involves being fully present and aware of one's thoughts, emotions, and actions while maintaining the focus and commitment necessary to achieve long-term goals. This approach not only helps in overcoming distractions and temptations but also promotes a deeper understanding of oneself and the motivations behind one's actions.

At the heart of mindful self-discipline is the practice of mindfulness. Mindfulness is the art of paying attention to the present moment without judgement. It involves being aware of your thoughts, feelings, and sensations as they arise, allowing you to respond to them consciously rather than reacting automatically. By cultivating mindfulness, individuals can develop greater self-awareness, which is essential for effective self-discipline.

One of the key benefits of mindful self-discipline is enhanced emotional regulation. When individuals are mindful, they are better able to observe their emotions without becoming overwhelmed by them. This awareness allows them to manage their reactions and make thoughtful decisions, even in stressful or challenging situations. For example, if someone feels the urge to procrastinate, mindfulness can help them recognize this urge, understand its underlying cause, and choose to stay focused on their task instead.

Mindful self-discipline also promotes clarity of purpose. By being present and fully engaged in the moment, individuals can gain a clearer understanding of their goals and the steps needed to achieve them. This clarity helps to prioritise tasks and allocate time and resources effectively. It also fosters a sense of intention, ensuring that actions are aligned with long-term objectives rather than being driven by short-term impulses.

Another significant advantage of mindful self-discipline is the ability to manage stress more effectively. Mindfulness practices, such as meditation and deep breathing, help to calm the mind and reduce stress levels. When combined with self-discipline, these practices enable individuals to maintain their focus and productivity even in the face of pressure. This resilience is crucial for sustaining long-term efforts and achieving meaningful goals.

Mindful self-discipline also encourages a compassionate approach to self-improvement. Instead of being harsh or overly critical when faced with setbacks, individuals practising mindful self-discipline learn to treat themselves with kindness and understanding. This self-compassion fosters a positive mindset, making it easier to stay motivated and committed to personal growth.

Incorporating mindful self-discipline into daily life involves several practical steps. Firstly, individuals can begin by setting clear, realistic goals and breaking them down into manageable tasks. This approach provides a structured plan and a sense of direction. Secondly, regular mindfulness practices, such as meditation, yoga, or mindful breathing, can help to develop greater self-awareness and emotional regulation. Thirdly, maintaining a routine that includes time for reflection and self-assessment can help individuals stay aligned with their goals and make necessary adjustments along the way.

Additionally, practising mindful self-discipline involves being aware of and managing distractions. This can include creating a conducive environment for focused work, setting boundaries with technology, and developing strategies to stay on track when distractions arise. By staying mindful of these factors, individuals can cultivate a disciplined approach that supports their long-term objectives.

In conclusion, the power of mindful self-discipline lies in its ability to combine the awareness and presence of mindfulness with the focus and commitment of self-discipline. This powerful combination enhances emotional regulation, clarity of purpose, stress management, and self-compassion. By incorporating mindful self-discipline into daily routines, individuals can achieve their goals more effectively, improve their overall well-being, and lead more fulfilling lives.

Self -discipline as a personal harmony

Self-discipline as a personal harmony represents a holistic approach to managing one's actions, emotions, and desires in a balanced and integrated manner. This concept views self-discipline not merely as a tool for achieving goals but as a means of creating a harmonious internal state where various aspects of one's personality and life are aligned and work together seamlessly. Here's an exploration of how self-discipline fosters personal harmony:

1. Alignment of Actions with Values
Self-discipline ensures that an individual's actions are consistent with their core values and long-term goals. This alignment creates a sense of integrity and coherence, reducing internal conflict and promoting a feeling of wholeness. When people act in ways that reflect their true values, they experience a deep sense of satisfaction and peace.

2. Balance Between Immediate and Long-term Goals
Self-discipline involves making choices that balance immediate desires with long-term objectives. This balance prevents the extremes of either constant

self-indulgence or rigid self-denial. By finding a middle path, individuals can enjoy the present while still working towards future goals, thus maintaining a harmonious lifestyle.

3. Emotional Regulation

Practising self-discipline helps in managing emotions effectively. It teaches individuals to respond to their emotions thoughtfully rather than reacting impulsively. This regulation leads to emotional stability, reducing stress and fostering a calm, composed state of mind that contributes to overall harmony.

4. Consistent Personal Growth

Self-discipline promotes continuous self-improvement. By setting and adhering to personal goals, individuals cultivate habits that lead to growth and development. This steady progress fosters a sense of achievement and fulfilment, reinforcing the harmony between one's present actions and future aspirations.

5. Integration of Mind and Body

Self-discipline often involves practices that nurture both the mind and body, such as regular exercise, healthy eating, and mindfulness meditation. These practices create a balanced, integrated approach to well-being, where physical health supports mental clarity and vice versa, leading to overall personal harmony.

6. Enhanced Focus and Productivity

By eliminating distractions and staying focused on important tasks, self-discipline increases productivity. This efficiency reduces the stress of unfinished tasks and the chaos of a cluttered schedule, creating a more orderly and harmonious daily life.

7. Positive Relationships
Self-discipline extends to interpersonal relationships, where it encourages behaviours such as active listening, patience, and empathy. These disciplined actions foster deeper, more meaningful connections with others, contributing to a harmonious social environment.

8. Self-Compassion and Resilience
A harmonious approach to self-discipline involves self-compassion. Recognizing and accepting one's imperfections and setbacks without harsh judgement fosters resilience. This kind approach ensures that self-discipline is sustainable and nurturing rather than punitive, leading to long-term personal harmony.

9. Purpose and Meaning
Finally, self-discipline helps individuals stay true to their purpose and find meaning in their actions. This sense of purpose provides direction and motivation, creating a unified and coherent life path that resonates with their inner values and desires.

Self discipline in your brain

Self-discipline is a mental skill rooted in specific brain functions and structures that help regulate behaviour, emotions, and decision-making processes. Understanding how the brain facilitates self-discipline can provide insight into how to strengthen this vital trait. Here are key aspects of self-discipline in the brain:

1. Prefrontal Cortex: The Executive Center

The prefrontal cortex, located at the front of the brain, is primarily responsible for higher-order functions such as decision-making, planning, impulse control, and goal-setting. This region is crucial for self-discipline because it enables individuals to:

- **Evaluate consequences:** Weighing the long-term outcomes of actions versus short-term rewards.

- **Plan and set goals:** Formulating and adhering to structured plans to achieve objectives.

- **Suppress impulses:** Controlling immediate desires or distractions to stay focused on tasks.

2. Anterior Cingulate Cortex: Conflict Monitoring

The anterior cingulate cortex (ACC) plays a role in monitoring conflicts between competing desires or actions. It helps in:

- **Error detection:** Recognizing when behaviour deviates from goals or standards.

- **Cognitive control:** Adjusting behaviour to align with goals and suppressing inappropriate responses.

3. Basal Ganglia: Habit Formation

The basal ganglia, a group of nuclei in the brain, are involved in habit formation and the automation of repeated behaviours. When self-discipline becomes habitual, the basal ganglia help:

- **Streamline routines:** Making disciplined actions automatic, requiring less conscious effort.

- **Reinforce positive habits:** Encouraging the repetition of beneficial behaviours through reward systems.

4. Dopamine System: Reward and Motivation

Dopamine is a neurotransmitter that plays a key role in the brain's reward and motivation systems. It influences self-discipline by:

- **Providing motivation:** Driving the pursuit of goals through the anticipation of rewards.

- **Reinforcing behaviour:** Strengthening the connection between disciplined actions and positive outcomes.

5. Amygdala: Emotional Regulation

The amygdala, part of the brain's limbic system, is involved in processing emotions, particularly fear and pleasure. Its role in self-discipline includes:

- **Emotional control:** Helping to manage emotional responses that could derail disciplined behaviour.

- **Stress response:** Regulating stress and anxiety that can impact decision-making and self-control.

6. Neuroplasticity: Adapting and Strengthening

Neuroplasticity is the brain's ability to reorganise itself by forming new neural connections. This adaptability is crucial for developing and enhancing self-discipline:

- **Learning and growth:** Strengthening neural pathways associated with disciplined behaviour through practice and repetition.

- **Adapting to challenges:** Adjusting strategies and responses as new challenges or goals arise.

Practical Strategies to Enhance Self-Discipline

Understanding the brain mechanisms behind self-discipline can guide practical strategies to strengthen it:

- **Mindfulness and meditation:** Practices that enhance the function of the prefrontal cortex and ACC, improving focus and emotional regulation.

- **Goal setting and planning:** Structured approaches that engage the prefrontal cortex, aiding in clear decision-making and impulse control.

- **Habit formation:** Repeatedly practising disciplined behaviours to leverage the basal ganglia's role in automating actions.

- **Reward systems:** Using positive reinforcement to enhance dopamine-driven motivation for maintaining disciplined actions.

- **Stress management:** Techniques such as deep breathing and exercise to regulate the amygdala's response to stress, ensuring better emotional control.

Chapter 2: The benefit of self discipline

Self-discipline is a foundational trait that brings numerous benefits to various aspects of life. By cultivating self-discipline, individuals can achieve their goals, improve their well-being, and foster better relationships. Here are some key benefits of self-discipline:

1. Achieving Goals

Self-discipline helps individuals stay focused on their long-term objectives, ensuring that short-term temptations do not derail their progress. This persistence is crucial for:

- **Academic success:** Consistently studying and completing assignments leads to better grades and deeper knowledge.

- **Career advancement:** Meeting deadlines, maintaining productivity, and continuously improving skills can lead to promotions and career growth.

- **Personal projects:** Whether it's learning a new hobby, writing a book, or starting a business, self-discipline ensures steady progress.

2. Improved Health and Fitness

Self-discipline is essential for maintaining a healthy lifestyle. It enables individuals to:

- **Adopt healthy eating habits:** Making consistent, healthy food choices instead of succumbing to junk food.

- **Exercise regularly:** Sticking to a workout routine, even on days when motivation is low.

- **Avoid harmful behaviours:** Resisting the urge to engage in activities such as smoking, excessive drinking, or drug use.

3. Better Emotional Regulation

Practising self-discipline helps individuals manage their emotions more effectively. Benefits include:

- **Reduced stress:** Staying organised and managing time effectively can prevent last-minute rushes and the stress they cause.

- **Enhanced resilience:** The ability to stay calm and collected in the face of challenges and setbacks.

- **Improved mood:** Regular exercise, adequate sleep, and healthy eating supported by self-discipline can lead to better mental health and overall mood.

4. Financial Stability

Self-discipline plays a critical role in managing finances wisely. It helps individuals:

- **Save money:** Consistently setting aside a portion of income for savings or investments.

- **Budget effectively:** Sticking to a budget and avoiding unnecessary spending.

- **Reduce debt:** Making regular payments to pay off debts and avoiding the accumulation of new debt.

5. Enhanced Productivity

With self-discipline, individuals can maximise their productivity. This includes:

- **Time management:** Prioritising tasks and allocating time effectively to complete them.

- **Focus and concentration:** Minimising distractions and maintaining attention on the task at hand.

- **Task completion:** Consistently finishing tasks and projects, leading to a sense of accomplishment.

6. Stronger Relationships

Self-discipline positively impacts personal and professional relationships by fostering:

- **Reliability:** Being dependable and meeting commitments builds trust with others.

- **Better communication:** Listening actively and responding thoughtfully in conversations.

- **Conflict resolution:** Staying calm and composed during disagreements, leading to more constructive resolutions.

7. Personal Growth

Self-discipline encourages continuous self-improvement and learning. Benefits include:

- **Skill development:** Regularly practising and honing new skills.

- **Self-awareness:** Reflecting on behaviours and making adjustments to align with personal values and goals.

- **Increased confidence:** Achieving goals and overcoming challenges builds self-esteem and confidence.

8. Greater Life Satisfaction

Ultimately, self-discipline contributes to a fulfilling and purposeful life. It allows individuals to:

- **Live with intention:** Making deliberate choices that align with personal values and long-term aspirations.

- **Experience balance:** Managing various aspects of life, such as work, health, and relationships, in a harmonious way.

- **Achieve fulfilment:** The satisfaction that comes from reaching goals, overcoming obstacles, and continuously growing.

Makes you confident and empowered

Self-discipline is a powerful trait that significantly contributes to building confidence and a sense of empowerment. By practising self-discipline, individuals can gain control over their lives, make consistent progress toward their goals, and develop a stronger sense of self-worth. Here's how self-discipline fosters confidence and empowerment:

1. Achievement of Goals

Self-discipline enables individuals to set and achieve their goals consistently. Each accomplishment, no matter how small, boosts confidence and reinforces the belief in one's abilities. The process of setting goals, making plans, and following through with them proves to oneself that success is attainable through effort and perseverance.

2. Improved Self-Efficacy

Self-efficacy is the belief in one's capability to execute tasks and achieve goals. Practising self-discipline helps build this belief by providing evidence of one's ability to control impulses, stay focused, and overcome challenges. This improved self-efficacy translates into higher confidence in tackling new and demanding tasks.

3. Enhanced Skill Development

Through disciplined practice and dedication, individuals can develop and refine their skills. Mastery of skills, whether professional, academic, or personal, leads to increased competence and self-assurance. Knowing that one has the ability and expertise to perform well in various areas of life is a significant confidence booster.

4. Consistency and Reliability

Self-discipline fosters consistency in actions and behaviours. Being reliable and consistent in meeting commitments and responsibilities builds trust and respect from others. This external validation reinforces one's self-esteem and sense of empowerment, knowing that others can depend on them.

5. Overcoming Obstacles

When individuals practise self-discipline, they learn to face and overcome obstacles rather than avoiding them. This resilience in the face of challenges instils a sense of strength and capability. Overcoming difficulties through disciplined effort provides a profound sense of accomplishment and empowerment.

6. Control Over Life Choices

Self-discipline empowers individuals by giving them control over their choices and actions. This control leads to a greater sense of autonomy and independence. When people feel in control of their lives, they are more confident in their decisions and less likely to be swayed by external pressures.

7. Reduced Stress and Anxiety

Practising self-discipline helps individuals manage their time, responsibilities, and emotions more effectively, leading to reduced stress and anxiety. A calm and composed mind enhances confidence, as individuals are better equipped to handle unexpected situations and make clear decisions.

8. Positive Self-Image

Consistently making disciplined choices that align with one's values and goals contributes to a positive self-image. When individuals see themselves as disciplined and capable, their self-esteem improves. This positive self-perception is a crucial component of overall confidence and empowerment.

9. Setting an Example

Being disciplined often inspires and influences others positively. When individuals see the benefits of their disciplined actions reflected in the success and respect they earn, it further boosts their confidence. Knowing that they can be role models and inspire others is empowering.

10. Long-Term Satisfaction

The sense of fulfilment that comes from achieving long-term goals through self-discipline leads to lasting satisfaction and pride. This deep-seated contentment fosters a stable and enduring confidence that is not easily shaken by temporary setbacks or failures.

Enable you to achieve your goals

Self-discipline is crucial for achieving goals as it provides the structure and persistence needed to navigate the path to success. Here's how self-discipline helps you achieve your goals:

1. Establishes Clear Objectives

Self-discipline begins with setting specific, realistic, and measurable goals. It helps you define what you want to achieve clearly and create a focused plan of action. This clarity ensures you know exactly what you need to work towards.

2. Creates a Structured Plan

With self-discipline, you can develop a detailed plan to reach your goals. This plan includes breaking down large goals into smaller, manageable tasks, setting deadlines, and establishing milestones. A structured plan keeps you organised and provides a roadmap for your journey.

3. Promotes Consistent Effort
Achieving goals requires regular and sustained effort. Self-discipline ensures that you consistently take the necessary actions and make progress, even when motivation fluctuates. This steady effort is essential for long-term success.

4. Enhances Focus and Concentration
Self-discipline improves your ability to stay focused on tasks. It helps you avoid distractions and maintain concentration on activities that directly contribute to your goals. This focus increases productivity and efficiency.

5. Overcomes Procrastination
Procrastination can derail progress towards your goals. Self-discipline helps you overcome the tendency to delay tasks by promoting a proactive approach and encouraging timely completion of responsibilities.

6. Manages Time Effectively
Effective time management is key to achieving goals. Self-discipline aids in prioritising tasks, allocating time appropriately, and avoiding time-wasting activities. This ensures that you dedicate sufficient time to important tasks and stay on schedule.

7. Builds Positive Habits

Self-discipline helps in developing and maintaining positive habits that support your goals. Consistent behaviours, such as regular exercise, healthy eating, or daily practice, become second nature, making it easier to stay on track.

8. Fosters Resilience and Persistence
Challenges and setbacks are inevitable on the path to success. Self-discipline fosters resilience and persistence, helping you to bounce back from difficulties, learn from failures, and continue working towards your goals.

9. Enhances Self-Control
Self-discipline involves managing impulses and making decisions that align with your long-term objectives. It helps you resist short-term temptations that could hinder your progress and stay committed to your goals.

10. Increases Accountability
Self-discipline encourages personal accountability. It involves taking responsibility for your actions and their outcomes, which motivates you to stay committed to your goals and adhere to your plan.

11. Allows for Adaptability
While self-discipline promotes adherence to plans, it also involves flexibility. When faced with unexpected changes, disciplined individuals can adapt their strategies and stay focused on their goals, ensuring continued progress despite obstacles.

12. Strengthens Long-Term Vision

Self-discipline supports maintaining a long-term perspective. By keeping your ultimate goals in view, you can make strategic decisions and endure short-term sacrifices, knowing they contribute to your overall success.

Gives you purpose, power, peace

Self-discipline provides a profound sense of purpose, power, and peace, enriching various aspects of life. Here's how each of these benefits manifests through self-discipline:

1. Purpose

Self-discipline helps you define and pursue your goals with clarity and commitment. It provides a sense of purpose by:

- **Clarifying Goals:** By setting and sticking to goals, self-discipline helps you identify what truly matters and what you want to achieve in life.

- **Creating Direction:** A disciplined approach to your tasks and responsibilities aligns your daily actions with your long-term objectives, giving you a clear direction and a sense of meaning.

- **Fostering Motivation:** Working consistently towards your goals enhances your sense of purpose, fueling your motivation and drive.

2. Power

Self-discipline empowers you to take control of your actions, decisions, and life circumstances. It gives you power by:

- **Boosting Confidence:** Successfully achieving goals and overcoming challenges through disciplined efforts strengthens your confidence and self-efficacy.

- **Enhancing Control:** By managing your impulses and making deliberate choices, you exert control over your life, shaping your path according to your values and ambitions.

- **Building Resilience:** Discipline equips you with the ability to handle setbacks and obstacles, reinforcing your power to persist and succeed.

3. Peace

Self-discipline contributes to a sense of inner peace by creating stability and reducing stress. It brings peace by:

- **Reducing Stress:** Effective time management and organisation reduce the chaos and pressure of last-minute efforts, leading to a more relaxed and manageable life.

- **Promoting Balance:** Discipline helps you maintain balance by integrating various aspects of life such as work, health, and relationships harmoniously.

- **Fostering Contentment:** The achievement of goals and the consistency of disciplined efforts bring a sense of accomplishment and satisfaction, leading to overall peace and contentment.

Chapter 3: Self discipline in daily life

Self-discipline in daily life involves consistently applying self-control and making deliberate choices to achieve your goals and maintain well-being. Here's how you can integrate self-discipline into various aspects of daily living:

1. Time Management

- **Create a Schedule:** Plan your day with specific time blocks for work, exercise, leisure, and rest. Stick to this schedule to enhance productivity and balance.

- **Set Priorities:** Identify and focus on high-priority tasks. Use techniques like the Eisenhower Matrix to distinguish between urgent and important activities.

2. Healthy Living

- **Follow a Routine:** Establish regular habits for eating, exercise, and sleep. Consistency in these areas supports physical health and well-being.

- **Set Goals:** Aim for specific health goals, such as exercising three times a week or reducing sugar intake. Track your progress and adjust as needed.

3. Work and Productivity

- **Avoid Procrastination:** Break tasks into smaller, manageable parts and set deadlines for each. Use techniques like the Pomodoro Technique to maintain focus and manage work time effectively.

- **Maintain Focus:** Limit distractions by creating a dedicated workspace and using tools like website blockers to stay focused during work hours.

4. Financial Management

- **Budgeting:** Create a monthly budget that tracks income, expenses, and savings. Adhere to this budget to manage finances effectively and avoid overspending.

- **Savings Plan:** Automate savings by setting up automatic transfers to a savings account. Aim to save a portion of your income regularly.

5. Personal Development

- **Daily Learning:** Allocate time each day for learning new skills or expanding your knowledge, such as reading books, taking online courses, or practising a new language.

- **Set Personal Goals:** Establish and work towards personal development goals, such as improving communication skills or developing a new hobby.

6. Emotional Regulation

- **Practice Mindfulness:** Engage in mindfulness techniques such as meditation or deep breathing exercises to manage stress and enhance emotional awareness.

- **Reflect Daily:** Spend a few minutes each day reflecting on your emotions and experiences. Journaling can help you process feelings and maintain emotional balance.

7. Relationships

- **Communicate Effectively:** Make a conscious effort to listen actively and respond thoughtfully in your interactions with others. Set aside quality time for meaningful conversations.

- **Set Boundaries:** Establish and maintain healthy boundaries to ensure balanced relationships and prevent overcommitment or burnout.

8. Habits and Routines

- **Build Positive Habits:** Focus on building habits that align with your goals, such as daily exercise, healthy eating, or reading. Start small and gradually increase the intensity.

- **Evaluate and Adjust:** Regularly review your routines and habits. Make adjustments as needed to stay aligned with your goals and improve your daily life.

9. Self-Care

- **Prioritise Rest:** Ensure you get adequate sleep each night to recharge and maintain overall health. Develop a bedtime routine that promotes restful sleep.

- **Engage in Relaxation:** Incorporate activities that help you unwind and relax, such as hobbies, walks, or spending time with loved ones.

10. Accountability and Reflection

- **Track Progress:** Use tools like planners, apps, or journals to monitor your progress towards goals and reflect on your achievements and areas for improvement.

- **Seek Feedback:** Engage with mentors, coaches, or peers for feedback and support to help you stay disciplined and motivated.

Mindful time management

Mindful time management integrates awareness and intention into how you allocate and use your time. It emphasises being present and deliberate with how you approach tasks and commitments. Here's how you can practise mindful time management effectively:

1. Set Clear Intentions

- **Define Priorities:** Start by identifying your most important tasks and goals. This helps ensure that you focus on what truly matters rather than getting lost in less significant activities.

- **Establish Goals:** Break down large goals into smaller, actionable tasks. Set clear, achievable objectives for each day or week.

2. Plan and Schedule

- **Create a Daily Schedule:** Use a planner or digital calendar to outline your day. Allocate specific times for tasks, breaks, and personal activities, ensuring a balanced approach.

- **Time Blocking:** Dedicate blocks of time to specific tasks or activities. This helps maintain focus and reduces the likelihood of multitasking, which can decrease productivity.

3. Practise Focused Work

- **Single-Tasking:** Focus on one task at a time. Complete it before moving on to the next. This approach minimises distractions and enhances the quality of your work.

- **Use the Pomodoro Technique:** Work for 25 minutes, then take a 5-minute break. After four cycles, take a longer break. This method helps maintain concentration and prevents burnout.

4. Monitor Your Time

- **Track Activities:** Use time-tracking tools or apps to monitor how you spend your time. This can help identify time-wasting habits and areas where adjustments are needed.

- **Reflect Regularly:** At the end of each day or week, review how you spent your time. Reflect on what went well and what could be improved.

5. Manage Distractions

- **Create a Distraction-Free Environment:** Minimise interruptions by setting up a dedicated workspace, turning off notifications, and letting others know your work times.

- **Practice Mindfulness:** When you find yourself getting distracted, gently bring your focus back to the task at hand. Techniques like deep breathing or a short mindfulness exercise can help.

6. Incorporate Breaks and Rest

- **Schedule Breaks:** Regular breaks are essential for maintaining productivity and mental well-being. Use breaks to relax, stretch, or engage in activities you enjoy.

- **Prioritise Rest:** Ensure you get adequate sleep and downtime. A well-rested mind is more focused and efficient.

7. Set Boundaries

- **Establish Work Hours:** Define clear work hours and stick to them. Avoid extending work into personal time to maintain a healthy work-life balance.

- **Learn to Say No:** Be mindful of your limits and avoid overcommitting. Saying no to additional tasks or responsibilities can help you stay focused on your priorities.

8. Practice Self-Compassion

- **Be Kind to Yourself:** Acknowledge that not every day will go as planned. Practice self-compassion when things don't go perfectly and adjust your plans as needed.

- **Celebrate Achievements:** Recognize and celebrate your accomplishments, no matter how small. This positive reinforcement can boost motivation and maintain a balanced perspective.

9. Optimise Your Routine

- **Morning and Evening Routines:** Develop mindful morning and evening routines to start and end your day with intention. This can set a positive tone for your day and help you wind down effectively.

- **Reflect and Adjust:** Regularly review your routines and time management strategies. Adjust them based on what works best for you and your evolving needs.

Clarify your priorities

Clarifying your priorities involves identifying what is most important to you and aligning your actions and decisions accordingly. Here's how to effectively clarify your priorities:

1. Reflect on Your Values

- **Identify Core Values:** Consider what matters most to you in life, such as family, health, career, personal growth, or community. Your values guide your priorities.

- **Assess Current Alignment:** Evaluate how well your current activities and commitments align with these values.

2. Set Specific Goals

- **Define Long-Term Goals:** Outline what you want to achieve in various areas of your life, such as career, relationships, and personal development. Ensure these goals reflect your values.

- **Break Down Goals:** Divide long-term goals into smaller, actionable steps. This makes them more manageable and helps you focus on what needs to be done first.

3. Evaluate Urgency vs. Importance

- **Use the Eisenhower Matrix:** Categorise tasks into four quadrants:

- **Urgent and Important:** Tasks that need immediate attention and contribute to long-term goals.

- **Important but Not Urgent:** Tasks that contribute to long-term goals but don't require immediate action.

- **Urgent but Not Important:** Tasks that need quick attention but don't significantly impact your goals.

- **Not Urgent and Not Important:** Tasks that neither require immediate attention nor contribute significantly to your goals.

- **Prioritise Accordingly:** Focus on tasks that are both urgent and important, and plan for tasks that are important but not urgent.

4. Assess Time and Energy

- **Analyse Your Schedule:** Look at how you currently spend your time and energy. Identify activities that align with your priorities and those that don't.

- **Adjust Allocations:** Reallocate time and energy to activities that support your key priorities, and minimise time spent on less important tasks.

5. Make a Prioritisation List

- **Rank Priorities:** Create a list of your top priorities based on your values and goals. Rank them to clarify which ones should receive the most attention and resources.

- **Regular Review:** Periodically review and adjust your priorities as needed based on changes in your life, goals, or circumstances.

6. Set Boundaries

- **Establish Limits:** Define clear boundaries to protect your time and energy for your top priorities. This might include setting work hours, avoiding overcommitment, or saying no to tasks that don't align with your goals.

- **Communicate Clearly:** Let others know your priorities and boundaries to ensure they respect your time and commitments.

7. Create a Plan of Action

- **Develop Actionable Steps:** For each priority, outline specific actions you need to take. Create a timeline or schedule to guide your efforts.

- **Track Progress:** Regularly monitor your progress towards your priorities and make adjustments as necessary to stay on track.

8. Reflect and Adjust

- **Regular Reflection:** Set aside time to reflect on your priorities and progress. Assess whether your current focus aligns with your goals and values.

- **Adapt as Needed:** Be flexible and adjust your priorities and plans based on new insights, experiences, or changes in your life.

Social influence

Social influence refers to the ways in which individuals' thoughts, feelings, and behaviours are affected by others. It encompasses a variety of mechanisms, including conformity, compliance, and obedience, which can significantly shape our decisions and actions. Understanding social influence is crucial for recognizing how external factors impact personal and collective behaviour.

Types of Social Influence

1. Conformity

Conformity occurs when individuals adjust their behaviour or beliefs to match those of a group. This can be due to:

- **Normative Influence:** The desire to be liked or accepted by others, leading to adherence to group norms.

- **Informational Influence:** The need to be correct, resulting in adopting the behaviours or opinions of others when uncertain.

2. Compliance

Compliance involves changing one's behaviour in response to a direct request from another person. Common techniques include:

- **Foot-in-the-Door:** Starting with a small request to increase the likelihood of agreeing to a larger one later.

- **Door-in-the-Face:** Making a large request that is likely to be refused, followed by a smaller, more reasonable request.

3. Obedience

Obedience is following orders or instructions from an authority figure. This type of influence is often studied in the context of authority and power dynamics.

Mechanisms of Social Influence

1. Persuasion

Persuasion involves changing attitudes or behaviours through communication and argument. Effective persuasion often relies on:

- **Credibility:** Trustworthiness and expertise of the source.

- **Attractiveness:** Physical appeal or likability of the persuader.

- **Message Framing:** Presenting information in a positive or negative light.

2. Social Proof

Social proof is the tendency to look to others to determine what is correct or acceptable, especially in ambiguous situations. This can manifest in behaviours like following trends or imitating peers.

3. Role Models

Role models influence behaviour by serving as examples. Observing the actions and successes of others can inspire similar behaviours in individuals.

Effects of Social Influence

1. Positive Effects

- **Encouraging Positive Behaviours:** Social influence can promote beneficial behaviours such as healthy eating, exercise, and academic achievement.

- **Enhancing Social Cohesion:** Shared norms and behaviours can strengthen group identity and cooperation.

2. Negative Effects

- **Peer Pressure:** Can lead to harmful behaviours, such as substance abuse or risky activities, especially among adolescents.

- **Groupthink:** The desire for harmony or conformity in a group can result in irrational or dysfunctional decision-making.

Factors Affecting Social Influence

1. Group Size
Larger groups often exert more influence, but very large groups may reduce the impact of individual influence.

2. Unanimity
The presence of a unanimous group opinion can significantly increase conformity and compliance.

3. Cohesion

Tighter-knit groups tend to have stronger social influence over their members.

4. Status and Authority

Individuals are more likely to be influenced by those with higher status or authority.

Strategies to Manage Social Influence

1. Awareness

Recognize when social influence is at play. Understanding the mechanisms can help resist unwanted pressure.

2. Critical Thinking

Evaluate the validity of the information and the motivations behind it. Question the norms and behaviours that are being promoted.

3. Assertiveness

Develop assertiveness skills to express your own views and make independent decisions confidently.

4. Seek Diverse Perspectives

Expose yourself to different viewpoints to avoid being overly influenced by a single group or authority.

Chapter 4: Meditation benefit for self discipline

Meditation offers numerous benefits for enhancing self-discipline, as it cultivates mindfulness, self-awareness, and mental resilience. Here's how meditation can improve self-discipline:

1. Enhanced Focus and Concentration

- **Improved Attention Span:** Regular meditation trains your mind to focus on a single point, such as your breath or a mantra. This practice can enhance your ability to concentrate on tasks and resist distractions.

- **Better Task Completion:** By improving your focus, meditation helps you stay on track with tasks and projects, reducing procrastination and boosting productivity.

2. Increased Self-Awareness

- **Understanding Habits:** Meditation fosters greater self-awareness, allowing you to recognize habitual behaviours and thought patterns that might undermine your self-discipline.

- **Mindful Choices:** With heightened self-awareness, you become more conscious of your choices, enabling you to make decisions that align with your goals and values.

3. Reduced Stress and Anxiety

- **Emotional Regulation:** Meditation helps in managing stress and anxiety by promoting relaxation and emotional balance. A calmer mind is better equipped to handle challenges and maintain discipline.

- **Decreased Impulsivity:** Lower stress levels lead to reduced impulsivity, making it easier to stick to your plans and resist temptations that could derail your progress.

4. Strengthened Willpower

- **Mental Resilience:** Meditation enhances your mental resilience by training your brain to stay calm and composed under pressure. This resilience is crucial for maintaining self-discipline in challenging situations.

- **Delayed Gratification:** Practising meditation strengthens your ability to delay gratification, a key component of self-discipline. It helps you prioritise long-term goals over short-term pleasures.

5. Improved Emotional Intelligence

- **Better Emotional Understanding:** Meditation increases your ability to understand and manage your emotions. This emotional intelligence allows you to navigate difficult situations without losing sight of your objectives.

- **Enhanced Relationships:** Improved emotional intelligence fosters better interpersonal relationships, reducing conflicts and distractions that can impede self-discipline.

6. Consistency and Routine

- **Habit Formation:** Incorporating meditation into your daily routine establishes a regular practice, reinforcing the habit of consistency. This consistency can spill over into other areas of your life, promoting disciplined behaviours.

- **Structure and Stability:** A regular meditation practice adds structure and stability to your day, making it easier to maintain other healthy routines and habits.

7. Mindful Living

- **Present Moment Awareness:** Meditation encourages living in the present moment, reducing the tendency to ruminate on past mistakes or future worries. This present-moment focus supports disciplined action in the here and now.

- **Intentional Actions:** With increased mindfulness, you become more intentional about your actions, aligning them with your long-term goals and values.

Practical Tips for Using Meditation to Boost Self-Discipline

- **Start Small:** Begin with just a few minutes of meditation each day and gradually increase the duration as you become more comfortable with the practice.

- **Consistency is Key:** Aim to meditate at the same time each day to build a consistent routine. Morning or evening sessions can be particularly effective.

- **Use Guided Meditations:** If you're new to meditation, guided sessions can help you stay focused and provide structure to your practice.

- **Combine with Goal Setting:** Use your meditation time to reflect on your goals and visualise the disciplined actions needed to achieve them.

- **Be Patient:** Developing self-discipline through meditation is a gradual process. Be patient with yourself and recognize that progress takes time.

what is hindering your discipline

Various factors can hinder self-discipline, making it challenging to stay focused and achieve your goals. Understanding these obstacles is the first step toward overcoming them. Here are some common hindrances to self-discipline and strategies to address them:

1. Lack of Clear Goals

- **Problem:** Without specific, well-defined goals, it's hard to know what you're working towards.

- **Solution:** Set SMART goals (Specific, Measurable, Achievable, Relevant, Time-bound) to provide direction and motivation.

2. Poor Time Management

- **Problem:** Inefficient use of time can lead to procrastination and missed deadlines.

- **Solution:** Use time management techniques such as creating schedules, setting priorities, and breaking tasks into smaller steps. Tools like calendars and to-do lists can help.

3. Distractions

- **Problem:** External distractions (like social media, noise) and internal distractions (such as daydreaming) can derail focus.

- **Solution:** Create a dedicated, distraction-free workspace. Use apps or tools to block distracting websites and practice mindfulness to improve concentration.

4. Lack of Motivation

- **Problem:** Without sufficient motivation, it's easy to lose interest and give up.

- **Solution:** Identify your "why" – the deeper reason behind your goals. Break tasks into smaller, rewarding milestones and celebrate progress to stay motivated.

5. Negative Habits

- **Problem:** Established negative habits can undermine efforts to build discipline.

- **Solution:** Replace negative habits with positive ones gradually. Use habit-tracking tools and reward systems to reinforce new behaviours.

6. Stress and Fatigue

- **Problem:** High stress levels and lack of rest can deplete energy and focus, making self-discipline harder to maintain.

- **Solution:** Prioritise self-care by ensuring adequate sleep, regular exercise, and relaxation techniques like meditation or yoga.

7. Perfectionism

- **Problem:** Striving for perfection can lead to procrastination or burnout, as tasks seem overwhelming.

- **Solution:** Adopt a growth mindset, focusing on progress rather than perfection. Break tasks into smaller, manageable parts and accept that mistakes are part of the learning process.

8. Fear of Failure

- **Problem:** Fear of not succeeding can prevent you from taking action or persisting with tasks.

- **Solution:** Reframe failure as a learning opportunity. Set small, achievable goals to build confidence and gradually tackle larger challenges.

9. Lack of Support

- **Problem:** Without a supportive environment or people who encourage your goals, maintaining discipline can be tough.

- **Solution:** Surround yourself with supportive friends, family, or mentors. Consider joining groups or communities with similar goals for mutual encouragement and accountability.

10. Low Self-Efficacy

- **Problem:** Doubting your ability to succeed can undermine your efforts and resolve.

- **Solution:** Build self-efficacy by setting and achieving small goals, practising positive self-talk, and reflecting on past successes.

11. Inconsistent Routines

- **Problem:** Irregular routines can disrupt the development of disciplined habits.

- **Solution:** Establish and stick to regular routines for work, exercise, meals, and sleep. Consistency helps build and maintain discipline.

12. Poor Planning

- **Problem:** Without a clear plan, it's easy to get sidetracked or overwhelmed.

- **Solution:** Plan your tasks and goals in advance. Use planners or digital tools to map out steps and deadlines.

13. Overcommitment

- **Problem:** Taking on too many tasks can lead to burnout and decreased discipline.

- **Solution:** Learn to say no to additional commitments that don't align with your primary goals. Focus on quality over quantity.

How to make your negative emotions work for you and not against you.

Harnessing negative emotions can transform them into powerful motivators rather than obstacles. Here's how to make them work for you:

1. Acknowledge and Accept

Recognize and accept your negative emotions without judgement. Understanding that it's normal to feel anger, fear, or sadness is the first step towards using them constructively.

2. Identify Triggers

Pinpoint what causes these emotions. Knowing your triggers helps you anticipate and manage your responses better, turning potential disruptions into opportunities for growth.

3. Channel Energy

Redirect the energy from negative emotions into productive activities. For example, use anger to fuel a workout or channel anxiety into meticulous planning and preparation.

4. Practice Mindfulness

Mindfulness helps you stay present and observe your emotions without becoming overwhelmed. Techniques like deep breathing and meditation can calm your mind and provide clarity.

5. Learn from Emotions

Treat negative emotions as signals that something needs attention. Reflect on what these emotions are telling you about your needs, values, or boundaries and take proactive steps to address them.

6. Reframe Your Perspective

Shift your mindset to see challenges as opportunities. Viewing setbacks as learning experiences can reduce the emotional burden and increase resilience.

By acknowledging, understanding, and strategically channelling negative emotions, you can turn them into catalysts for personal growth and improved self-discipline.

Daily habits to improve self-discipline

Improving self-discipline involves cultivating daily habits that reinforce focus, consistency, and control. Here are some effective habits:

1. Set Clear Goals
Begin each day by outlining your goals. Clear, specific goals provide direction and motivation, helping you stay focused on what matters most.

2. Create a Routine
Establish a consistent daily schedule. Having a structured routine reduces decision fatigue and promotes productive habits.

3. Prioritise Tasks
Use the Eisenhower Matrix to prioritise tasks based on urgency and importance. Focus first on what's most crucial to achieve your long-term goals.

4. Practice Mindfulness

Incorporate mindfulness techniques like meditation or deep breathing. Mindfulness enhances self-awareness and helps manage stress, improving your ability to stay disciplined.

5. Limit Distractions

Identify and minimise distractions in your environment. Use tools and apps to block distracting websites and set specific times for checking emails and social media.

6. Exercise Regularly

Engage in physical activity daily. Exercise boosts mood, energy levels, and cognitive function, all of which support better self-discipline.

7. Reflect Daily

End your day with reflection. Review what you accomplished, what challenges you faced, and how you can improve tomorrow. Reflection fosters continuous improvement.

8. Get Adequate Sleep

Ensure you get enough rest each night. Quality sleep is essential for maintaining focus, energy, and decision-making abilities.

By integrating these habits into your daily routine, you can steadily enhance your self-discipline, leading to greater productivity and personal fulfilment.

Chapter 5: Creating a discipline

Creating self-discipline involves developing habits and strategies that reinforce your ability to stay focused, manage your time, and achieve your goals consistently. Here's a comprehensive guide to building self-discipline:

1. Set Clear, Achievable Goals

- **Define Your Objectives:** Start with specific, measurable, achievable, relevant, and time-bound (SMART) goals. Clear goals provide direction and motivation.

- **Break Down Goals:** Divide larger goals into smaller, manageable tasks. This makes them less overwhelming and easier to tackle.

2. Develop a Routine

- **Consistent Schedule:** Establish a daily routine that includes time for work, exercise, meals, relaxation, and sleep. Consistency helps form habits and reduces decision fatigue.

- **Morning and Evening Routines:** Start your day with a positive morning routine to set the tone, and wind down with an evening routine to reflect and prepare for the next day.

3. Prioritise Tasks

- **Use the Eisenhower Matrix:** Categorise tasks by urgency and importance to prioritise effectively. Focus on high-priority tasks first to make significant progress.

- **Daily To-Do Lists:** Create a list of tasks for each day, ranked by priority. This keeps you organised and ensures you address essential tasks.

4. Manage Time Efficiently

- **Time Blocking:** Allocate specific time blocks for different activities. This helps maintain focus and prevents multitasking.

- **Set Deadlines:** Assign deadlines to tasks to create a sense of urgency and ensure timely completion.

5. Minimise Distractions

- **Create a Focused Environment:** Designate a quiet, clutter-free workspace. Use tools and apps to block distracting websites and notifications.

- **Limit Multitasking:** Focus on one task at a time to improve quality and efficiency.

6. Practice Mindfulness

- **Meditation and Deep Breathing:** Incorporate mindfulness practices to enhance self-awareness, reduce stress, and improve focus.

- **Regular Breaks:** Take short breaks to rest and recharge. Techniques like the Pomodoro Technique can help maintain productivity.

7. Exercise Regularly

- **Physical Activity:** Include regular exercise in your routine. Physical activity boosts mood, energy, and cognitive function, supporting better discipline.

8. Reflect and Adjust

- **Daily Reflection:** Review your accomplishments and challenges at the end of each day. Reflecting helps identify areas for improvement.

- **Learn from Mistakes:** View setbacks as learning opportunities. Adjust your strategies and continue moving forward.

9. Seek Accountability and Support

- **Accountability Partner:** Find someone to share your goals and progress with. Regular check-ins can motivate you to stay on track.

- **Join a Group:** Engage with communities or groups that share similar goals. Mutual support and encouragement can enhance discipline.

10. Practice Self-Compassion

- **Be Kind to Yourself:** Understand that building self-discipline is a gradual process. Celebrate small victories and forgive yourself for setbacks.

- **Positive Reinforcement:** Reward yourself for meeting milestones. Positive reinforcement can boost motivation and encourage continued progress.

By implementing these strategies consistently, you can cultivate strong self-discipline, enabling you to achieve your goals and lead a more productive and fulfilling life.

Minimising distractions

Minimising distractions is vital for enhancing self-discipline. Here are effective strategies:

1. Create a Focused Environment

- **Dedicated Workspace:** Choose a quiet, clutter-free area specifically for work or study to limit external distractions.

- **Ergonomics and Comfort:** Ensure your workspace is comfortable to maintain concentration without physical discomfort.

2. Use Technology Wisely

- **Block Distractions:** Utilise apps like Freedom or StayFocusd to block distracting websites and manage notifications during focused periods.

- **Scheduled Checks:** Designate specific times for checking emails and social media to avoid constant interruptions.

3. Time Management Techniques

- **Time Blocking:** Use techniques like the Pomodoro Technique to allocate focused work periods followed by short breaks.

- **Prioritise Tasks:** Tackle high-priority tasks first to stay aligned with your goals.

4. Set Boundaries

- **Communicate Availability:** Inform others of your work hours to minimise interruptions.

- **Consistent Routine:** Establish and stick to a routine that reinforces productive habits.

By implementing these strategies, you can significantly reduce distractions, thereby strengthening your self-discipline and improving productivity.

Resilience

Resilience is the capacity to recover quickly from difficulties and adapt well in the face of adversity, trauma, tragedy, threats, or significant sources of stress. It involves a combination of behaviours, thoughts, and actions that can be developed and strengthened over time. Key aspects of resilience include:

1. Emotional Regulation: Managing strong emotions and impulses.

2. Optimism: Maintaining a positive outlook and seeing challenges as opportunities.

3. Self-efficacy: Believing in one's ability to influence events and outcomes.

4. Problem-solving skills: Effectively addressing and resolving issues as they arise.

5. Social Support: Having strong, supportive relationships.

6. Adaptability: Being flexible and adaptable to change.

Resilience can be nurtured through various strategies, such as fostering connections, maintaining a healthy lifestyle, setting realistic goals, and seeking help when needed.

Protect your time

Protecting your time involves setting boundaries and prioritising tasks to ensure that your most important activities and responsibilities are given the attention they need. Here are some strategies to help protect your time:

1. Set Clear Priorities: Determine what tasks and activities are most important and focus on them first.

2. Learn to Say No: Politely decline requests that don't align with your priorities or that would overextend you.

3. Schedule Time Blocks: Allocate specific times for different tasks and stick to your schedule as much as possible.

4. Limit Distractions: Minimise interruptions by turning off notifications, setting specific times to check emails, and creating a dedicated workspace.

5. Delegate Tasks: Assign tasks to others when possible to free up your time for more critical activities.

6. Take Breaks: Schedule regular breaks to rest and recharge, which can improve overall productivity.

7. Set Boundaries: Establish clear boundaries between work and personal time to ensure a healthy work-life balance.

By implementing these strategies, you can better manage your time, reduce stress, and increase productivity.

Chapter 6: Crafting a self-discipline mindset

Crafting a self-discipline mindset involves developing habits and attitudes that enable you to consistently pursue your goals, even when motivation wanes. Here are some key strategies:

1. Set Clear Goals: Define specific, measurable, attainable, relevant, and time-bound (SMART) goals to give you direction and purpose.

2. Break Down Tasks: Divide larger goals into smaller, manageable tasks to avoid feeling overwhelmed and to make progress more tangible.

3. Create a Routine: Establish a daily schedule that includes dedicated time for your priorities and stick to it consistently.

4. Stay Organized: Keep a to-do list or use productivity tools to track tasks and deadlines.

5. Eliminate Temptations: Remove distractions and environments that hinder your ability to focus.

6. Practise Delayed Gratification: Learn to prioritise long-term benefits over immediate pleasures by setting rewards for completing tasks.

7. Build Accountability: Share your goals with others or work with an accountability partner to stay on track.

8. Develop Resilience: Embrace setbacks as learning opportunities and maintain a positive attitude toward challenges.

9. Stay Healthy: Ensure you get enough sleep, eat well, and exercise regularly, as physical well-being impacts mental discipline.

10. Reflect and Adjust: Regularly review your progress, reflect on what works and what doesn't, and adjust your strategies accordingly.

By integrating these practices into your daily life, you can develop a mindset that fosters self-discipline and helps you achieve your long-term goals.

Mindful shift

A mindful shift involves consciously redirecting your focus and attention to the present moment, fostering awareness and reducing stress. Here are steps to achieve a mindful shift:

1. Pause and Breathe: Take a few deep breaths to centre yourself and bring your attention to the present.

2. Observe Without Judgement: Notice your thoughts, feelings, and physical sensations without trying to change or judge them.

3. Ground Yourself: Use grounding techniques such as feeling your feet on the floor, noticing the sensation of your breath, or observing your surroundings.

4. Redirect Focus: Consciously shift your attention to what you are doing or experiencing in the moment.

5. Practice Gratitude: Reflect on things you are grateful for to cultivate a positive mindset.

6. Engage Fully: Immerse yourself in the current activity, whether it's work, a conversation, or a simple task like washing dishes.

7. Use Reminders: Set reminders or use cues to bring yourself back to mindfulness throughout the day.

8. Be Kind to Yourself: Practise self-compassion and avoid self-criticism when your mind wanders.

9. Regular Practice: Incorporate mindfulness practices, such as meditation, into your daily routine to strengthen your ability to shift mindfully.

By regularly practising these steps, you can develop the habit of making mindful shifts, enhancing your focus, reducing stress, and improving overall well-being.

Self Talk

Self-talk refers to the internal dialogue that runs through our minds throughout the day. It can significantly impact our mood, behaviour, and overall mental health. Positive self-talk can boost confidence, enhance performance, and improve overall well-being, while negative self-talk can lead to anxiety, depression, and decreased motivation.

To harness the power of positive self-talk, start by becoming aware of your thoughts. Notice when you engage in negative self-talk and challenge those thoughts. Replace them with more constructive and positive statements. For example, instead of thinking, I can't do this, reframe it to, I can try my best and learn from the experience.

Use affirmations to reinforce positive beliefs. Phrases like I am capable,I am resilient, and I can handle challenges can build a more optimistic mindset. It's also helpful to speak to yourself with the same kindness and encouragement you would offer a friend.

Practice gratitude and focus on your strengths and achievements rather than dwelling on shortcomings. Over time, consistent positive self-talk can reshape your mental patterns, leading to a more empowered and resilient approach to life's challenges. By nurturing a positive internal dialogue, you can foster a healthier, more productive mindset.

The power of routine

The power of routine lies in its ability to bring structure, efficiency, and stability to our lives. Here are some key benefits of establishing a routine:

1. Increased Productivity: By following a consistent schedule, you can better manage your time and accomplish more tasks efficiently. Routines help eliminate decision fatigue, allowing you to focus on what truly matters.

2. Reduced Stress: Knowing what to expect each day can alleviate anxiety and create a sense of control. A predictable routine reduces uncertainty and helps manage daily responsibilities with less stress.

3. Improved Mental Health: Regular routines can support mental well-being by incorporating time for self-care, relaxation, and hobbies. They also help in establishing healthy habits, like regular exercise and sufficient sleep.

4. Enhanced Focus and Discipline: Consistency in routine helps build self-discipline and reinforces good habits. It reduces procrastination and distractions, enabling you to stay focused on your goals.

5. Better Physical Health: A routine that includes regular exercise, balanced meals, and adequate sleep promotes overall physical health. Consistency in these areas is key to long-term wellness.

6. Goal Achievement: Routines break down large goals into manageable steps, making it easier to track progress and stay motivated. Daily habits contribute incrementally to achieving long-term objectives.

7. Work-Life Balance: Establishing boundaries between work and personal time helps maintain a healthy balance, preventing burnout and ensuring time for relaxation and relationships.

By creating and adhering to a routine, you can optimise your daily life, foster positive habits, and enhance your overall well-being.

Chapter 7: Surround yourself with the right people

Surrounding yourself with the right people is crucial for personal growth and well-being. The company you keep can significantly influence your mindset, behaviour, and success. Here are some key benefits of being around positive, supportive individuals:

1. Motivation and Inspiration: Positive and driven people can inspire you to set higher goals and strive for excellence. Their success stories and encouragement can fuel your ambition and persistence.

2. Emotional Support: Supportive friends and family provide a safety net during tough times. They offer empathy, understanding, and encouragement, helping you navigate challenges more effectively.

3. Constructive Feedback: Honest and constructive feedback from trustworthy individuals can help you improve and grow. They can point out areas for development and celebrate your achievements.

4. Healthy Habits: Being around people who prioritise health and wellness can encourage you to adopt similar habits. This includes regular exercise, healthy eating, and mindful practices.

5. Positive Influence: The right people foster a positive environment, reducing stress and negativity. They help cultivate an optimistic outlook, boosting your mental and emotional health.

6. Network and Opportunities: Surrounding yourself with accomplished and well-connected individuals can open doors to new opportunities, whether in your career or personal life.

By choosing to spend time with those who uplift, inspire, and support you, you create a foundation for a fulfilling and successful life.

Taking control of your mind

Taking control of your mind involves cultivating mental discipline, self-awareness, and positive thinking. Here are some strategies to help you achieve this:

1. Mindfulness and Meditation: Practising mindfulness and meditation helps you become aware of your thoughts and emotions without judgement. This awareness allows you to respond thoughtfully rather than react impulsively.

2. Positive Self-Talk: Replace negative thoughts with positive affirmations. Challenge and reframe unhelpful beliefs by focusing on your strengths and achievements.

3. Set Goals and Prioritise: Clearly define your goals and prioritise tasks that align with them. This focus helps eliminate distractions and maintain mental clarity.

4. Mental and Physical Health: Regular exercise, a balanced diet, and sufficient sleep are crucial for maintaining a healthy mind. Physical well-being directly impacts mental health and cognitive function.

5. Learning and Growth: Engage in activities that stimulate your mind, such as reading, solving puzzles, or learning new skills. Continuous learning keeps your mind sharp and adaptable.

6. Stress Management: Develop effective stress management techniques, such as deep breathing, yoga, or hobbies that relax and rejuvenate you. Reducing stress enhances mental control.

7. Limit Negative Influences: Avoid environments and people that contribute to negative thinking. Surround yourself with positive influences that support your mental well-being.

8. Seek Professional Help: If needed, don't hesitate to seek help from a mental health professional. Therapy or counselling can provide valuable tools and strategies for taking control of your mind.

By implementing these practices, you can cultivate a resilient, focused, and positive mindset, enabling you to navigate life's challenges with greater ease and confidence.

How to develop mental force

Developing mental fortitude involves building resilience, discipline, and a positive mindset. Here are key strategies to enhance your mental strength:

1. Embrace Challenges: View obstacles as opportunities for growth. Facing difficulties head-on helps build resilience and confidence in your abilities.

2. Cultivate a Positive Mindset: Focus on positive self-talk and reframe negative thoughts. Emphasise your strengths and achievements, and practice gratitude daily.

3. Set Realistic Goals: Break down larger objectives into manageable steps. Achieving small, consistent milestones boosts confidence and reinforces discipline.

4. Practice Mindfulness: Engage in mindfulness and meditation to increase self-awareness and reduce stress. Being present helps manage emotions and maintain focus.

5. Develop Healthy Habits: Regular exercise, a balanced diet, and sufficient sleep are essential for mental and physical well-being. Healthy habits enhance cognitive function and emotional stability.

6. Learn from Failure: View setbacks as learning experiences rather than failures. Analysing and understanding your mistakes fosters growth and resilience.

7. Seek Support: Surround yourself with positive, supportive people. Share your goals and challenges with trusted friends or mentors who can provide encouragement and constructive feedback.

8. Stay Adaptable: Flexibility in thinking and approach helps you navigate change and uncertainty. Being open to new ideas and adjusting your strategies is key to mental strength.

By consistently applying these strategies, you can build a robust mental foundation, enabling you to handle life's challenges with greater strength and determination.

Emotions and Self control

Emotions and self-control are deeply interconnected, influencing how we navigate life's challenges and interact with others. Developing self-control over your emotions involves understanding, managing, and effectively responding to your feelings. Here are some strategies to enhance emotional self-control:

1. Self-Awareness: Pay attention to your emotions and identify what triggers them. Understanding the root causes of your feelings is the first step in managing them effectively.

2. Mindfulness and Meditation: Regular mindfulness practice helps you stay present and aware of your emotions without being overwhelmed by them. Meditation can increase emotional regulation and reduce stress.

3. Pause and Reflect: When you feel strong emotions, take a moment to pause before reacting. This brief pause allows you to think through your response rather than acting impulsively.

4. Breathing Techniques: Deep breathing exercises can help calm your mind and body, making it easier to manage intense emotions. Practise slow, deep breaths to regain composure.

5. Positive Self-Talk: Replace negative thoughts with positive affirmations. Encourage yourself with constructive and kind words, which can help shift your emotional state.

6. Healthy Outlets: Engage in physical activity, creative pursuits, or hobbies to channel your emotions constructively. Physical exercise, in particular, can reduce stress and improve mood.

7. Set Boundaries: Establish boundaries to protect your emotional well-being. This may involve limiting exposure to stressful situations or toxic individuals.

8. Seek Support: Talk to friends, family, or a therapist about your emotions. External support can provide perspective and help you develop better coping strategies.

9. Practice Empathy: Understanding others' emotions and perspectives can improve your emotional intelligence and help you respond more thoughtfully.

10. Continuous Learning: Read books or attend workshops on emotional intelligence and self-control. Continuous learning can provide new techniques and insights for managing emotions.

By incorporating these strategies into your daily life, you can develop greater self-control over your emotions, leading to improved relationships, better decision-making, and overall enhanced well-being.

Chapter 8: Organising yourself

Organising yourself is essential for cultivating self-discipline. Here's how effective organisation supports and enhances self-discipline:

1. Establish Clear Goals

- **Define Objectives:** Clearly outline your goals and break them into smaller, manageable tasks. Specific goals provide direction and make it easier to stay focused.

- **Set Deadlines:** Assign deadlines to tasks to create a sense of urgency and accountability.

2. Create a Structured Routine

- **Daily Schedule:** Develop a daily schedule that allocates time for work, exercise, and relaxation. Consistent routines reinforce disciplined behaviour and prevent procrastination.

- **Prioritise Tasks:** Use tools like the Eisenhower Matrix to categorise tasks by importance and urgency. Focus on high-priority tasks first.

3. Utilise Time Management Techniques

- **Time Blocking:** Dedicate specific time blocks for focused work and breaks. This technique helps maintain concentration and prevents burnout.

- **Pomodoro Technique:** Work in intervals (e.g., 25 minutes) followed by short breaks. This method improves focus and productivity.

4. Organise Your Workspace

- **Declutter:** Keep your workspace tidy and free from distractions. An organised environment fosters better focus and efficiency.

- **Accessible Resources:** Use filing systems, digital tools, and storage solutions to keep materials organised and easily accessible.

5. Use Tools and Apps

- **Task Management:** Utilise apps like Todoist or Trello to track tasks, set reminders, and manage deadlines. These tools help maintain organisation and accountability.

- **Calendar:** Use digital calendars to schedule and manage appointments, deadlines, and daily activities.

6. Implement Consistent Routines

- **Morning and Evening Routines:** Establish routines for starting and ending your day to build momentum and reinforce discipline.

- **Weekly Planning:** Spend time each week reviewing goals, planning tasks, and adjusting schedules as needed.

7. Regular Review and Reflection

- **Daily Reflection:** Assess your progress each day, identify successes, and address any challenges.

- **Weekly Review:** Evaluate your weekly achievements, adjust plans, and prepare for the upcoming week.

By organising your goals, routines, workspace, and tools, you enhance your ability to stay disciplined and focused, making it easier to achieve your objectives and maintain consistent progress.

The mental barrier to self discipline

Mental barriers to self-discipline often stem from internal conflicts, limiting beliefs, and emotional challenges that undermine your ability to stay focused and achieve goals. Understanding and addressing these mental barriers can significantly improve your self-discipline.

1. Procrastination

Procrastination involves delaying tasks despite knowing their importance. It's often driven by fear of failure, perfectionism, or feeling overwhelmed. To overcome procrastination, break tasks into smaller steps, set clear deadlines, and use techniques like the Pomodoro Technique to create a structured approach.

2. Lack of Motivation

Low motivation can hinder self-discipline, making it difficult to start or persist with tasks. This often results from not connecting tasks to personal values or long-term goals. To boost motivation, clearly define the why behind your goals and find ways to align tasks with your interests and values.

3. Fear of Failure

Fear of failure can paralyse action and prevent you from pursuing goals. This fear often stems from a lack of confidence or past negative experiences. Reframe failure as a learning opportunity and build self-efficacy by setting and achieving smaller, manageable goals to build confidence.

4. Perfectionism

Perfectionism can lead to unrealistic expectations and excessive self-criticism, making tasks seem daunting. This can result in procrastination or avoidance. Embrace a growth mindset, focus on progress rather than perfection, and set realistic, achievable standards.

5. Lack of Self-Awareness

Without self-awareness, you may not recognize the patterns and triggers that undermine your discipline. Develop self-awareness through mindfulness practices, journaling, and reflecting on your habits and behaviours to identify and address these barriers.

6. Negative Self-Talk

Negative self-talk can erode confidence and self-discipline. Challenge negative thoughts with positive affirmations and evidence of past successes. Practice self-compassion and focus on constructive self-feedback to foster a more supportive inner dialogue.

7. Emotional Regulation

Difficulty managing emotions such as stress, anxiety, or frustration can affect self-discipline. Incorporate stress-management techniques like mindfulness, exercise, and relaxation exercises to improve emotional regulation and resilience.

Addressing these mental barriers involves a combination of practical strategies and psychological self-awareness. By tackling these internal obstacles, you can strengthen your self-discipline and enhance your ability to achieve your goals.

Developing morning and evening action plans

Developing structured morning and evening action plans is a key strategy for enhancing self-discipline. These plans help create routines that promote productivity, focus, and overall well-being. Here's how to design effective morning and evening action plans:

Morning Action Plan

1. Start with a Consistent Wake-Up Time

- Set a Regular Alarm: Wake up at the same time each day to regulate your body's internal clock and build a consistent routine.

2. Morning Routine

- Hydrate and Stretch: Begin with a glass of water and some light stretching to energise your body.

- Mindfulness or Meditation: Spend 5-10 minutes practising mindfulness or meditation to set a positive tone for the day.

3. Set Priorities

- Daily Goals: Review your goals for the day. Identify 2-3 key tasks to focus on that align with your long-term objectives.

- To-Do List: Create or review your to-do list, prioritising tasks by importance and urgency.

4. Healthy Habits

- Exercise: Incorporate some form of physical activity, whether a workout, a walk, or yoga, to boost energy and focus.

- Healthy Breakfast: Eat a balanced breakfast to fuel your body and mind.

5. Prepare for the Day

- Plan Your Schedule: Review your calendar and schedule appointments, meetings, and work blocks.

- Organise Workspace: Ensure your workspace is organised and ready for productive work.

Evening Action Plan

1. Wind Down Routine

- Unwind: Spend 10-15 minutes unwinding from the day. Engage in a relaxing activity such as reading, light stretching, or listening to calming music.
- Limit Screen Time: Avoid screens at least an hour before bed to improve sleep quality.

2. Reflect on the Day

- Review Achievements: Reflect on what you accomplished during the day. Celebrate small victories and acknowledge progress.

- Identify Challenges: Note any challenges faced and consider strategies for overcoming them in the future.

3. Prepare for Tomorrow

- Plan Next Day's Tasks: List tasks and priorities for the following day. This helps create a sense of readiness and reduces morning stress.

- Set Goals: Define 1-2 key goals for the next day to stay focused and motivated.

4. Establish a Sleep Routine

- Consistent Bedtime: Go to bed at the same time each night to ensure adequate rest.

- Create a Relaxing Environment: Maintain a cool, dark, and quiet sleeping environment to improve sleep quality.

5. Practice Gratitude

- Gratitude Journal: Spend a few minutes writing down things you are grateful for. This practice fosters a positive mindset and can improve overall well-being.

By implementing these morning and evening action plans, you can create a structured framework that supports self-discipline, enhances productivity, and fosters a balanced lifestyle.

developing mental toughness

Developing mental toughness is crucial for strengthening self-discipline. Mental toughness involves resilience, focus, and the ability to overcome challenges, all of which support sustained discipline. Here's how to cultivate mental toughness to enhance self-discipline:

1. Set Clear Goals

- Define Objectives: Set attainable, quantifiable, and precise goals. Having well-defined goals gives you focus and drive, which supports your discipline even during difficult situations.

2. Build Resilience

- Accept Challenges: See challenges as chances to improve. Instead of running from obstacles, adopt a problem-solving mentality when you encounter them.

Learn from Failure: Consider past mistakes to see what went wrong and how to move forward. Make the most of setbacks as teaching opportunities to fortify your determination.

3. Develop a Growth Mindset

- Positive Self-Talk: Swap out negative ideas for encouraging remarks and constructive criticism. Think about how you can develop and get better with work.

Celebrate Progress: Acknowledge and rejoice in little accomplishments. This boosts your confidence and reaffirms your devotion.

4. Practice Self-Control

- Control Impulses: Create plans to withstand sudden cravings that go against your long-term objectives. Distraction and mindfulness are two strategies that can support attention retention.

- Establish Routines: Make sure your daily schedule is regular and in line with your objectives. Routines help create habits and lessen the need for ongoing judgement.

5. Strengthen Focus

- Establish Top Priority Tasks and Concentrate on Them: Decide on priorities. Avoid multitasking since this could impair focus and reduce productivity.

- Cut Down on Distractions: Eliminate distractions from within and outside the room to create an environment that promotes attention.

6. Enhance Emotional Regulation

- Practice Mindfulness: To reduce stress and preserve emotional equilibrium, practice mindfulness. Methods such as deep breathing and meditation assist you in maintaining your composure under duress.

Make the decision to improve your self-control right now. Establish precise objectives, establish a disciplined schedule, and take on obstacles head-on. Take action today, maintain concentration, and turn your potential into reality.

Conclusion

Self-discipline is a crucial trait that enables people to overcome challenges and accomplish their goals. By establishing well-defined goals, instituting organised schedules, and skillfully handling interruptions, you cultivate a resilient mindset that propels achievement. Self-discipline is cultivated because it turns potential into achievement and promotes both professional and personal development.

www.ingramcontent.com/pod-product-compliance
Lightning Source LLC
Chambersburg PA
CBHW071946210526
45479CB00002B/833